MERCENARY AT MIDNIGHT

A Collection of Gutsy Verse by

Nicholas Ryan Howard

PRAISE FOR MERCENARY AT MIDNIGHT

"Nicholas Ryan Howard's collection is at times unconventional and often emotionally raw-edged, all while revealing a lithe earnestness. Taking turns being conversational and directional, the poems collect into a kind of novena, a recurring group of prayers venerating the author's experience in the realms of love and lust, of creation and destruction, of heaven and hell on earth. His choice to weave the fantastical into the explicitly temporal gives the reader a chance to reflect on their own experiences and emotions following along with the wry spirit of the inherent storytelling. *Mercenary at Midnight* is at once a dark path in a deep forest and a cocktail on a streetside patio in a busy metropolis—and wherever you find it takes you—that is expressly where you are meant to be."

- Rosa Nadine Xochimilco Sánchez, author of *Blue Bones, Blood Roses, Black Eyes* and *Hearts Aflame, Still Burning*

"Nicholas Ryan Howard's verse is the definition of mastery and skill. *Mercenary at Midnight* grants its readers an up close and personal look into his life's journey through all of its love and pain, and he never shies away from vulnerability. His words are carefully crafted, yet still provide a relatable experience that will allow you to tap into your own heart's journey."

- Julisa Wilson, rapper and songwriter

"*Mercenary at Midnight* is unfiltered, raw, sensual, tactile, and untethered in its complete dismissal of self-justification. These are poems that leave us questioning our own motives, and echoing our unadorned desires. Nicholas Ryan Howard explores the anxiety of love and the dangerous brutality of idealism, moving seamlessly through the gambit of human experience. He is all at once proud, insecure, helpless, tortured, hot-headed, ashamed, and depleted—yet never afraid of a fight. He writes in the tone of a man on the second floor of a burning building.

"A journey with this self-proclaimed 'Midnight Mercenary' will bring any reader a cathartic reward for their time spent wide-eyed and face-first in the fields of harsh human realities. Face your fears and go into battle alongside this gifted wordsmith to receive your spoils of war."

- Kaitlin Weichsel, musician and host of the *Show Me Yours* poetry event in Hollywood, CA

ISBN: 978-1-7328878-4-8
KDP - Paperback - v01d

Edited by Rosa Nadine Xochimilco Gevaux in collaboration with Xochimilco Press.
Cover Artwork by Nicholas Ryan Howard with photography by Jack Nolan. Photo taken during a live reading at the "Show Me Yours" poetry event in Hollywood, CA hosted by Kaitlin Weichsel.
Audiobook music by Deborah Lurie.
Audiobook sound engineering by Karen Yee.
Author photo by Keegan Allen.

MORE ABOUT THE AUTHOR

www.NicholasRyanH.com
@NicholasRyanH

MORE ABOUT THE COLLECTION

www.MercenaryAtMidnight.com
@MercAtMidnight

The Audiobook

This collection of verse is also available in the audio format featuring powerful readings of each piece by the author.

Nicholas Ryan Howard has performed his work at readings and events around the world, and his performances are filled with vigor, honesty, and vulnerability.

The audio is an excellent companion to the written word and enables the listener to hear the unique rhythms and rhyming schemes intended for the material.

Now available.

TABLE OF CONTENTS

Dedicated to everyone I've hurt.
Balancing on that razor's edge between selfless
and self-honoring, I've drawn far too much blood.

Part One

BROKEN LOVE

*Relentless reflections of a raging,
raucous, ravaged heart.*

HEARTBREAK

Heartbreak

is feeling absolutely nothing

and absolutely everything

at the speed of light

while time

stands

still.

He'll lie to you
break you in two
and crush your joy
his little toy
and you, you'll pine
for scraps of time.
Because it's hot to need.

You can't be blamed,
you've ascertained.
It's not just you
he's done it to.
The other doves
he's made his loves
are proof that he's pure steam.

On you he'll flex
with calls for sex
that you'll allow
and wonder how
a man can be
so quick to see...
Who else is up tonight?

But with each thrust
of succumbed lust,
and cavalier
crack to the rear,
you've fed a beast
another feast,
and strengthened his resolve.

You've made it fine
for him to dine
upon the skin
of every whim.
And he'll endure
eyeliner blurred
across your teary face.

For what you fuck
don't give a fuck.
And that good ride
takes for a ride
a weaker soul
that has a hole.
No thrust will fill that void.

I think in Angel, but I speak Demon.

CRYSTAL

You sparkle like crystal...
...shattered on the street.
A thousand glints
crunching
under feet.

You smell of red roses...
...petals dried through.
Wilted
in a bowl
drained of hue.

Your voice is a song...
...the volume too low.
All treble,
no bass.
Played out. No tempo.

Your body's like heaven...
...all prayers and no sin.
A tithe
for valueless
virtue within.

Your eyes are like fire...
...the flame all but gone.
So lukewarm.
No more light.
Always dusk. Never dawn.

MASCARA

Your smile
it beams
like a thousand suns
that blotch out
and fade down
as mascara runs.
I can't allow
such expression
to burn.

Not without me.
Not without me.

Your hand
it fits
like a glove
from a store
that millionaires
and billionaires
just adore.
But that shit
shouldn't fit
on the small
of his back.

What about mine?
What about mine?

Your bliss
it smells
like a fresh baked pie
that grandma baked
to bring you joy.
It's sweetness
on his tongue
must taste divine.

But not on mine.
But not on mine.

Your eyes
so pure
so honest
so sure
must be ripped out
and stomped on
and blinded
and scorned.
Because they see
what you shouldn't see.

Please see me.
Please see me.

OCEAN

An ocean wild,

ravaging shores,

roaring a declaration of might,

could not deter

the thought of you

and my need to brave the night.

DRAGON

Never kiss a dragon,

for though they taste of passion,

they'll leave you charred

and smoked

and scarred

and make your heart

so ashen.

ANGER

Love fills

but anger

engulfs.

EMPTY

When a warmth
fills the empty—
what
does it
become?

A languid
creeping
light—
a virus
that consumes
the cold.

The heat is ravenous
merciless
greedy
an impetuous lover—
who never,
no never,
says
no.

TORCH

I'll flay it.
Slay it.
Kill it dead.

I'll torch it.
Scorch it.
Lop off its head.

I'll ice it.
Slice it.
Run it through.

This terrible,
horrible,
crush on you.

ANGEL

They called her an angel.
She was anything but.

She was a thief...
...who stole my heart.

She was a strangler...
...who took my breath away.

She was a pusher...
...who forced me to fall for her.

I should have known.
Angels don't drink whiskey.

IMPURE

Your fella treats you right.
He takes you out at night.
He buys you things
and diamond rings
and smiles at you so bright.

He's so handsome and so kind.
He doesn't tax your mind.
He's safe and nice
and will suffice
for bank accounts combined.

This coupling's mature.
Congrats, you're now secure.
But fucked up love's
what I'm made of.
Come here. Let's be impure.

SIREN

A gaze so hot
my kneecaps froze.
A gaze so swift
its wind still blows.

A look so right
all else was wrong.
The look was sung
just like a song.

A glance so kind
all else seemed cruel.
This queenly glance
made me the fool.

Acknowledgment
was my downfall.
This siren's song's
a banshee's call.

I am an animal
so pour me chamomile
it's up to you
to sedate me
from taking you.

I am a dynamo
fierce every time you know
born in the wild
with the wolves
you can calm me though.

Don't let me be a beast
with teeth
when all I want to do is sit here nicely
with my tea.

Don't tempt me with your eyes
or your sighs
or once again you'll hear
my carnal cries.

I'm seeing spots
and my vision's gone blurry
now please let me taste you
or witness my fury.

It isn't right girl
you don't want it this way
you don't want a devil
you want me to behave.

Don't let me be a beast
with teeth
when all I want to do is be a good guy
with my tea.

Don't tempt me with your hips,
fingertips,
or once again you feel
my feral lips.

STOLEN

Stolen

always

tastes

better.

APPEAR

Why

even

appear

just

to

dis-

appear?

CHOKED

I
have
never
choked
on
my
words.

But
I
have
choked
on
yours.

The lake of dreams,
the gemstone's gleams,
the peaceful prayer,
the sun-kissed air...
All not the prize
from cloudless skies.
It's your eyes.
It's your eyes.

The rose's glow,
the talk of snow,
the sea of glass,
the domes of brass...
All not the gift
from breezes swift.
It's your art.
It's your heart.

FEAR

Your fingers
on your phone
on your cheek
on your face...

...take me to
another place.

Your hair
on your head
on your neck
I must kiss...

...leads me to
that state of bliss.

The soul
in your eyes
in your fierce
human form...

...creates in me
a raging storm.

For you are there
across from me.
But you and I
will never be.

My heart is weak
when you are near.
Approaching you
is my greatest fear.

The flames within

are neutered sin.

They scorch my skin

with "could have been."

They taste so thin

like watered gin.

And drive me to the brink.

No words spoken

hurts so much more

than the worst ones.

Your silence

is tantamount

to a coffin's nails.

She may be an angel...
the way she sings and smiles.

Or maybe she's a devil...
her mischief wraps for miles.

She's gentle, kind and gracious...
so demure. So polite.

But her sense of humor...
it's sharp, like Satan's bite.

I want to hold her sweetly...
in a soft and feather bed.

But there's no time for that shit...
she's painting the world red.

QUAKE

You and me
we'll be so free,
we'll quake the earth
just wait, you'll see.

You and I
will fly so high,
we'll break right through
earth's fragile sky.

You and me
won't bend the knee,
we'll torch the rules
and burn decree.

You and I
won't wave goodbye,
to those who guzzled
every lie.

GUIDE

There's fire on the breeze,

and lust, it wets the seas.

The sizzles on your skin

are mountain peaks of sin.

The torment flows like wine,

and fiendishness tastes fine.

Don't fear, I'll be your guide

into the other side.

FOOL

Joy
is
a
child
that
gets
its
way.

Joy
is
a
fool
that's
in
my
way.

BEAUTY

I hate beauty.

It tortures me.

Taunts me.

Shows me my flaws.

Shows me my faults.

"My family is beautiful. I'll protect it."

"My religion is beautiful. I'll enforce it."

"My life is beautiful. I'll defend it."

Beauty begets brutality.

AWAY

Every time I love
I regret it.

Every time I succumb
I sweat it.

Every time I want
I don't get it.

Every inch of desire
I've bled it.

So fuck it.
Get rid of it.
Take it.

Away.

CANVAS

My lover's kiss
upon your skin.
A romance true,
a taste of sin.

The wind, it blows
upon your hip.
A storm in port,
for my lost ship.

The iron locked
upon your thigh,
it anchors me
to heaven's sky.

Through needle's sting
you bled your heart.
A canvas wet,
a work of art.

LIES

Did you teach

your eyes

to sell

such lies?

Just know

my ears

heed not

your tears.

CLUES

Are you a mystery
if you're leaving
no clues?

Are you a gamble
if there's nothing
to lose?

Are you a risk
if the truth's on
your face?

Is this a conquest
if the thrill's in
the chase?

REAL

Nice.
Nice is a joke.
Nice is a hideous joke.

He is nice.
She is nice.
They are nice.

Nice and plain.
Nice and passive.
Nice and resigned.
Nice and obedient.

What a nice doormat.

Kindness is different.

Kindness is real.

RIGHT

I

loved

you

right.

Right

into

the

arms

of

another

man.

VOICE

A voice in words
so musical in dreams.

A sudden jolt
into a state
of sound.

Eyes of gemstone
cool my heat
and warm what's cold
with only

a word.

I want.
I want her.
She's my new everything.

I want her face in my eyes.
I want her neck in my teeth.
I want to hold her and protect her.

And yet,
still devour her.

I want to ruin her.
I want to ruin her for others.

I want to ruin her and destroy her
so completely that she forgets about everything, and
everyone,
but me.

What am I.
Dear god, it hurts.

I am a beast.
A savage beast.

I want to destroy what I find beautiful?
I want to ruin what I find perfect?

Why.

Why.

I want to enter.
I want to last.

I want to see the whites in her eyes.
I want to leave claw marks down her back.

I want to destroy the world around me,
that fucking asshole world,
for putting anything in my way
that keeps me from clenching her
so hard
she turns
red.

I'll squeeze her until she bursts.

I don't care.

What the fuck am I?

I'd kill her with my love.
I'd suffocate her with my body.
I'd choke her with my passion.

Dear god.

Please.

Keep her the fuck away from me.

Don't let her near me.
I can only destroy her.
I can only destroy.

I can only consume her.
I was bred to consume.

I am a beast.

I am a beast.

I am a beast.

PASSION

Comfort

is,

"Love you."

Passion

is,

"Damn you."

ALLURE

Your form, it sickens me.

It's vile.

You're so proud of it.

Look at you.

The way you walk.

The way you squawk.

You're a monster in a dress.

Demanding want.

Demanding duels.

Demanding it all.

Your allure is a black hole.

SPIRITS

Spirits never linger.
They long to soar,
and answer calls,
that beckon new.

Spirits never linger.
They long to fly,
and feel the feels,
of heartbeats true.

How foolish of I
to wish them here,
for far they've gone
without my voice.

How foolish of I
to need them here,
for off they've gone
without my choice.

IMPERFECTION

Let me fill

your perfect eyes

with my perfect

imperfection.

TUESDAY

I wish anybody

loved me

in my lifetime

as much as you

love him

on a Tuesday.

SHATTER

I

can't

not

stomp

and

not

break

and

not

shatter

all

which

is

meant

to

be

safe

and

sound.

TOXIC

There is

nothing

fucking

worse

than the incredible feeling

of letting

something

toxic

go.

STONES

You are a polished stone.
A perfect gem
of rose and gold.
With these little blue sparkles
that no one
can't
not
see.

And I...
...I'm coal.
Of char and oil.
My form
of function
which won't
inspire
desire.

When someplace
put us side by side.
You gleamed your gleam
I did not hide.
I tried to gleam
but failed
because
I'm coal.

It was divine
you at my side.
And to myself
I deeply lied.
A piece of coal
with delusions of
a life
with a
gem.

For who would want
what makes you black
and smudged and rough
and chipped and cracked?
A polished stone
needs not
a lump
of coal.

And when we touched
it was enough
for me to see
how wrong it was.
I'll never be
a hunk
of chiseled
stone.

I'll always be
that which you're not,
a dirty rock
which when gets hot,
he lights,
ignites,
combusts,
and burns
aflame.

ENVY

Your beauty,
like lips brushing lips,
like a whisper of bliss,
like rose petal champagne,
will crumble
and wilt
and decay.

I'll laugh when it does,
a joyous laugh
of desperate relief,
as it means
my envy
may
now
sleep.

ZINFANDEL

You kiss me nice,
a heaven's slice...
but I just want some hell.

So smooth we lay,
like chardonnay...
but I want zinfandel.

You're kind to me,
so safe are we...
but I want this safe cracked.

You touch me light,
calm in the night...
but I must be attacked.

Though you were great,
and worth the wait...
I'll wait a little more.

For sizzling skin,
for red hot sin...
it's bore that I abhor.

DRUG

I've never

done a

drug

quite

like

you.

WRITHES

The crowd it sways,
and writhes and grinds,
your body moves,
my eyes it blinds.
But you don't give
a fuck
a damn
about me
about me.

A pulsing beat
makes rhythms rise
and crashes, smashes
hips to thighs.
But you can't give
a care
a shit
about me
about me.

Ecstasy swells
all horns and teeth.
But yet I dwell
in worlds beneath.
And you just gave
a bullet
dodged
to me
to me.

I

hate

the

way

you

love

me.

GUILE

I did what's right,
I shared my light.
I held you tight,
your eyes were bright.
But then one night,
you chose to spite me
and twist words and neck.

You felt my skin,
you kissed my chin.
I entered in,
such divine sin.
My new linchpin
you could have been but
rage hid in your soul.

Against your heart,
against your art,
you tore apart
this new fresh start.
And now depart
like horse sans cart but
still you're saddled to

your lies of pain,
your lust for gain,
your severed vein,
your lock and chain.
The way you feign
for sun through rain is
fiction, myth and guile.

To live for the pain

means love's gonna hurt.

THIRST

It is not gentle, the way you enter through my eyes.

Not a cool sensation.
Not a refreshing drink from a crystal lake.
Not a kind comfort.
Not a campfire on an already warm evening.

It is a sledgehammer to the corneas.
A violation.
A battering ram.
A steel-toed boot to a dead-bolted door
leaving a mess of wood-chips and splinters.

Your essence is lava.
An ooze of searing syrup.
A scalding chemical that flows down
behind my eye sockets, through my skull,
and into my heart,
leaving a sizzling trail, all the way.

And once the sight of you reaches my heart,
it ignites into a fire.
An unquenchable thirst.
An untamable, unrelenting churning of flame.
One explosion after another of why... why... why...

Why is God so cruel as to make someone like you,
impossible for someone like me to envelop?

Why has something so perfect for me, and only me,
been touched by another, been explored by another, and
been cast aside by another?

Why do you continue to assault me with your perfection,
your imperfection,
and your terrifying ability to send my serene days into a
tailspins of wretched yearning?

No, it is not gentle, the way you enter my eyes.

It is torture. A horrendous torture.

Don't stop.

YOU

In

the darkness,

there's a light.

It's you.

You,

the darkness

bright.

COFFEE

Light grows dark
and young grows old.
Which once was bright
is now less bold.

Yet...

The sting subsides,
the hurt doth slow.
When gifted with
a cup 'o joe.

Part Two

PARABLES OF CIRCUMSTANCE

Revelatory tales born of the macabre, the mighty, the minuscule and the magnificent.

HEROES

Villains take lives.

Heroes give theirs.

Villains are righteous.

Heroes are fair.

Villains pull triggers.

Heroes bond ties.

Villains die in vain

while more Heroes rise.

SEE

In those eyes
I see
a dream.

In that dream
I see
a hope.

In that hope
I see
a fear.

In that fear
I see
a need.

In that need
I see
a void.

In that void
I see
a chance.

POTION

This potion makes you kind.

This potion breaks your mind.

This potion's hot,

this potion's fraught

with powers undefined.

This potion knows your fears.

This potion spans the years.

This potion's free,

for you and me.

Known by the name of "Tears."

GOLD

If I could fly
I'd break the sky.
I'd be the why
the angels cry.
I'd get so high
I'd say goodbye
to every fucking thing.

The house of lies,
mistrusting eyes,
the faux surprise
when honor dies,
the time that flies
toward our demise
and splits our desperate hearts.

For we may hope
and we may dream
and we may pray
and we may sing,
but when it's time
to feel sublime
our souls are hollowed out.

We traded joy
for one more toy.
We bought the ploy
that we'd enjoy
if we'd destroy
each girl and boy
who never sucked the teat

of freedom's ring,
of thee we sing,
of stars and stripes,
and foreign gripes,
the sucking dicks,
of hypocrites
and swallowing their gold.

And bullshit here
and bullshit there
and gagging on
what they deem fair.
But we've endured
our vision blurred
from what's shot into our eyes.

For while we're blind
and hands are tied
we'll think upon
the times you lied,
and sharpen spikes,
and stockpile pikes,
inside our ravaged guts.

So sleep at night
with doors locked tight
and cuddle with your
platforms white
and male and straight
and 'Murca great
while we get hard for war.

MOON

I think the sun
would fight the moon
should they be found
in the same room.

Though one loves dark
and one loves light
and both could be
described as bright.

I do not think
they'd get along
on days so short
and nights so long.

Yet maybe they
would hug and kiss
for tensions built
may lead to bliss.

LONELINESS

A fool

covets

loneliness.

A coward

runs

from it.

ORATION

Resounding calls
of mirth with girth,
they stab unguarded hearts.

For past we see
of walls built tall,
defending weakened parts.

And those that jest
from places blessed,
and gossip with the tarts,

they weep inside
a wail that coats
oration that departs.

HELPING

Helping a friend

make a sane choice

is a responsible act

that demonstrates

both one's cowardice

and their cruelty.

TIRED

I'm so tired of fighting.
Of pushing through every blocked passage.
Of breaking down every locked door.

We've built a world of hoops,
to be jumped through,
at specific times,
in specific orders.

Orders.
Orders to be given.
Orders to be followed.

How rare it is
to hear the words, "Come on in,"
or, "You're welcome here,"
or, "Sure, why not."

It's a fight,
such a fight,
for the god given right
to hear such words.

TEETH

This

life

won't

have

teeth

'cause

I'll

have

kicked

them

all

in.

STORM

The eye

of the storm

sees peace

while the rest

of its body

destroys.

BLACK

In the trees I see the breeze
the gentle rustle of the leaves
I beg for peace, I'm begging please
but all I feel is black.

I spy the clouds, the soft, white shrouds
they travel slow, they travel proud
I long for joy, amongst their crowds
but all I know is black.

And in my soul I feel the cold
the nightfall grows and thickens bold
but heart and mind I do not scold
because I love the black.

It holds me.
And it whispers to me.
And it tempts me.
And I let it.

Because I love it.

GRAB

You stole from me,
and took what's mine.
You had to know
what's on the line.

A selfish grab
at what I loved:
a gift who came from
up above.

It isn't fair
you made this end,
and struck from earth
a dearest friend.

You'll never know
how much it hurts,
you petty, shitty
universe.

SHREDS

I'll torch these fucking walls.

I'll slice them all to shreds.

I'll shatter them,

and break their boards,

and rip out every thread.

SQUALL

I'll go up in smoke

by risking it all.

At least I made clouds

to rise above squall.

I'll go down in flames

by risking it all.

At least I made fire

to torch the cabal.

There's darkness in the light.

There's lightness in the dark.

Don't force me out of one,

don't push me into another.

Help me see it all.

DOOR

I'm one of two in a room of black,
a room with just one door.
A door that leads to the outside world,
a world with heart and wonder.

The other man inside this box,
how little he has seen.
For he was born inside this place
and lives in fear of dream.

I'm the blessing for this man,
his ticket to a life:
a job, a home, a chance for joy,
and possibly a wife.

This man, he's frail. He's cold, he's pale.
He's terrified of change.
He has no clue the room he's in
is keeping him in chains.

"All you have to do is go through the door," I say.
"Please don't make me," he responds.

It's just a door. A simple door.
A door so nondescript.
But the other side... such wondrous sights!
His spirits will soon lift.

I put my hand upon his back,
so warm and reassured.
I smile and sing and smile and swing
my hands and say these words:

Mercenary at Midnight

"All you have to do is go through the door."
"Please don't make me," he pleads.

But I know what's best! I've seen the rest!
The world so full of sights!
It's colorful and bright and bold,
and filled with city lights.

The opposite of black and cold.
His room will just not do.
I know I'm right, I know what's best.
This man just needs a clue.

"All you have to do is go through the door," I say.
"Please don't make me," he begs.

My patience starts to wear real thin,
my head, it starts to swim.
This man, he's daft. He's lost his mind.
He's goofy to the brim.

My hand of love, it starts to clench
the man right on the arm,
and gets real firm and pressure builds,
and loses all its charm.

"Just go through the door," I insist.
"Please don't make me," he cries.

He's going through, he has no choice!
The new world he will see!
And overcome with clarity
he'll hug and embrace me.

He'll laugh his silliness away
with tears and such relief,
and realize he was so wrong
about his own belief.

"All you have to do is go through the door," I say.
"Please don't make me. Please!"

But now my hand had turned to fist,
and anger filled my heart.
How rude he was! And ignorant
for fearing this fresh start.

I've been outside! I know it's best!
I know he's fully wrong!
He'll die in here, alone and cold...
unless he'll come along.

My fist, it trembled with regret
at what I next had done,
I struck the man. Right in the face.
Both he and I were stunned.

"All you have to do is go through the door!"
"Please, no..."

I threw the door open.
It slammed against the wall.
There were flowers. And air.
And clouds. And streams.

"Go through the fucking door!" I scream,
"because I know what's best!
I swear to Christ and God above
you'll put me to the test!"

He cried and wept and sobbed and wailed.
He shook and shook and shook.
I grabbed his arm and pulled him out,
next to a babbling brook.

I slammed the door. It went away.
It disappeared right then.
He ran for it. He cried and screamed,
and howled and shook again.

"Please, I want to go back," he whimpered.
"There is no going back. This is your life now."
He fell to the ground and wept.

He shunned the sky, the clouds,
the birds. Refused the grass and trees.
He simply sobbed and asked me why,
and begged upon his knees.

He wanted to go back to his life
of simple, bleak, and black.
A life he lived in ignorance,
but sans provoked attack.

I broke this man by forcing him
toward what he did not want.
I broke myself with violence.
The blow, my dreams will haunt.

For in my quest to grant him life
and truly set him free,
all I did was trade his chains
for a new form of slavery.

SEA

These waters cold,
these waters rough,
these waters off the map...

I'll sail them for you.
I'll sail them for you.

Though you may be iceberg,
though you may be siren,
though you may be lighthouse light...

I'll journey far,
I'll journey hard,
I'll journey out to sea.

Meet me there,
I know not where,
somewhere

way out
to
sea.

MONSTERS

The monster grinned it's grin of grins,
its teeth so clean and white.
It dusted off it's silky skin
of scales so gray and bright.

It took deep breaths and smiled so big
and practiced chewing up
all the things that it would eat
once grown up from a pup.

For it was young—but growing big—
and craving more new blood
to suck and fuck and twist around
and stomp on in the mud.

The other monster showed its claws,
then took him to their lair
which smelled of freshly polished bones
and maidens oh so fair.

This was the biggest monster club,
a place so full of screams,
and violence of every kind
which haunted all our dreams.

A place the little monster could use
to get so much more food,
though monster habits must be calmed—
it mustn't act so rude.

The king of the big monster crew
had nestled in his throne,
and eyed the little monster pup
and stared as tough as stone.

"Why do you wish to join our pack
and be with all the rest?
The biggest players in the game,
the best of all the best?"

The little monster showed it's tongue
and spewed a stream of puke.
Words like vomit poured like wine.
It acted like a Duke.

"I want to know of your past deeds,
and challenges you've hurdled.
The ways you've grown and shown your grit
and losers you have circled."

The puppy monster answered quick,
as quick as it could muster.
It laughed and snarled and made up shit,
it's talk all filibuster.

"Your words are good," the alpha spoke,
"though maybe should be quicker.
Initiative is what we crave,
not pensive, slow shit-kickers."

The little monster ran his mouth
a million miles an hour.
It growled with greed, its hunger huge,
and showed its lust for power.

"It's time you showed your love of us.
It's time to demonstrate
your knowledge of our pristine crew,
and all the ways we're great."

The pup, it spouted off its words
which sounded as they should.
It gleaned and gloated, noted, quoted,
every way it could.

"If you join us, it's for life.
Our ladder you must climb.
Where do you think you see yourself
with us in five year's time?"

The little monster made it known
its loyalty was true,
but asked of all the perks and ways
its dreams it could pursue.

For though 'twas drooling for a pride,
a way to get more meat,
it knew of other packs around.
This offer might be beat.

"I'm afraid we don't discuss salary until the second interview.
Next!"

SWEAT

Dreaming

is

Blood.

Building

is

Sweat.

Rebuilding

is

Tears.

If the wound

is where

the light

enters,

perhaps

my job

is to be

the

knife.

JUDGMENT

I'm sorry

I passed

judgment.

I'll try to

move past

judgment.

SIXTEEN

Fifteen people
and a box.
And this box
is full of rocks.
It won't budge
not with this flock.
To move it needs sixteen.

Here I am
to lend a hand.
Which makes these folks
a cheerful band.
With me
it's sure to go as planned.
To move it needs sixteen.

Charles, he frets.
He doesn't think
I shouldn't not have
made a stink.
He needs it all,
the kitchen sink.
To move it needs sixteen.

Edna also
makes a fuss
at how I smile at
all of us.
We shouldn't joke,
nor laugh, nor cuss.
To move it needs sixteen.

Jen, she frowns
and shakes her head.
"I'm glad to help,"
I should have said
according to
what's in her head.
To move it needs sixteen.

"We're really grateful
for your arms,"
says Tyler with
his suspect charms.
And frowns
when my heart doesn't warm.
To move it needs sixteen.

Brad, he wants
to move away.
"You shouldn't help
for just one day.
It's not enough,
this one short stay!"
To move it needs sixteen.

"It's plenty, Brad,"
Lee-Ann retorts.
But now she's very
out of sorts.
And now her temper's
getting short.
To move it needs sixteen.

"Our dad, he used
to help like this,"
said little Fran,
my little sis.
"Don't be like him,"
she then insists.
To move it needs sixteen.

But John, his dad
was never there.
"Pop never helped,"
he did declare.
"It's weird to have
this wound laid bare."
To move it needs sixteen.

When I offered
all my might,
it triggered Kitty's
sense of right.
"You shoulda first
put up a fight."
To move it needs sixteen.

Cameron saw just
one thing wrong:
he didn't like the choice of song
I liked to sing while
being strong.
To move it needs sixteen.

"I'm strong enough!"
said Carly-Sue.
"I swear I have
the strength of two!
I'm pretty sure
we don't need you."
To move it needs sixteen.

"I'm pretty sure
that he's just here
so Trisha will
buy him a beer.
His motives
aren't really clear."
To move it needs sixteen.

Karla stomps and
frets and slams
her fist, which rattles
glass and cans.
She curses us,
and us she damns.
To move it needs sixteen.

"Let's do it now,"
says Mary Mae.
"While we have
the light of day.
I'm positive
this is the way."
To move it needs sixteen.

"Wait for the dark,"
says snarky Fred,
"till sun is down
and gone to bed.
This heat right now
may make us dead."
To move it needs sixteen.

"It is a gift,
me being here."
Big John does say,
and gives a leer.
"Say thank you,
or in me you'll fear."
To move it needs sixteen.

So fifteen people
curse and fight
at how my help
must be *just right*.
The box, it did not move
that night.
To move it needs sixteen.

DROUGHT

How

is

there

a

drought

with

so

many

tears

to

go

around?

I'll sail the ocean of tears.

For though the sea may be salty,

this makes the shores sparkle.

REBIRTH

Alas, the wind

flows freely.

A cool warmth returns

to rebirth

the vigor

from

the venerable.

LEGACY

Oh you can tell by the way I fly,
and shriek and cry, refuse to die,
I'm not the man you think I am.
I'm not a squash-ed fly.

I shake and break and earthly quake,
and stay awake to sprint this lake,
that's made of ice but cracking nice.
A broken, freezing hell.

I hate to love, it breaks my heart
to be so kind and full of mind,
to give a break to all that take
my kindness for the norm.

They smile real big, such selfish pigs,
who grab at me and hope to be
one of the few, the chosen who
will ride my cresting wave.

But when shit's real, and pain I feel,
and things are dark, and there's no spark,
they run from me, and chastise me,
and hide inside their caves.

Where were you then? Where are you now?
Just wait until I take my bow
for praise I've earned, and lessons learned,
while you were jacking off

onto your life, onto your wife,
onto the lies you fetishize,
and when you're dry, and taste your lie,
I'll laugh at all you've done.

To buy your house, and wreck your spouse,
and birth the child you'll raise so mild,
and make like you, a clone of who
you need to feel alive.

You ghosted me, but here's the thing.
A ghost comes back and will attack
your thoughts and schemes and nightly dreams.
A ghost was born to haunt.

So screw your righteous faux concern.
I'll watch it break. I'll watch it burn.
And rest assured I'll rub it in,
for I've made peace with sin.

And fuck your bliss, it tastes like piss.
And screw your shit, you hypocrite.
Your legacy? A sellout's heart.
While I'm still making art.

Dragged me through hell.

From grace I fell.

Destroyed my life.

Nothing but strife.

Made pain the norm.

An endless storm.

This sexy thing called art.

PERFECTION

I have tasted perfection.

It is bittersweet.

PLEASE

My people are the bent.
My people are the broken.
My people are the ones who
are gutted but outspoken.

My people give their souls.
My people give their light.
My people are the ones who
brave every darkened night.

My people break the rules.
My people burn shit down.
My people are the ones
who rebel against the crown.

If your life is calm,
oh so filled with grace and ease,
you ain't one of my kind.
And if you think you are, bitch, please.

ONE

He loves the world and all its charms,
he smiles and sings with open arms,
the joy abounds, and his heart warms...
...he only hates just one damn thing.

Her life is great, her life is grand,
she takes sweet children by the hand,
she loves the beach, the surf, and sand...
...she only hates just one damn thing..

They swear they're fine, they swear they're good,
they do exactly as they should,
they'd bring world peace, you know they would...
...they only hate just one damn thing.

He's justified in this small hate,
it's no big deal, he's not irate,
on this please simply don't fixate...
...he only hates just one damn thing.

It's true, she'd wish that they weren't here,
when she sees them, why, she steers clear,
if only they would disappear...
...she only hates just one damn thing.

That color skin, it rubs them wrong,
If only they could get along,
But they all know they don't belong ...
...they only hate just one damn thing.

His grandma may have died.
Her husband may have lied.
Their pup is sick.
He came too quick.
There's no more sense of pride.

Her mother is a bitch.
His machine has a glitch.
They lost a friend.
Reached a dead end.
Fucked over by the rich.

And though we find it vile
when folks ain't chipper all the while,
don't be a twit.
They're going through shit.
And don't owe a returned smile.

DEMONS

I no longer battle my demons.

They know I don't fight fair.

LOST

Lost all his friends. He's in deep.

Doesn't fear God. He fears sheep.

Can't accept help. That slope's steep.

Insists he's awake. We're asleep.

The country's a mess. It's a heap.

That woman in charge? She's a creep.

His vow to his race? That he'll keep.

Millions like him? Makes me weep.

Thunder quivers
at my fist
which ignites flame
like Satan's kiss.

Windstorms cower
at my eyes
that break the seams
of clever lies.

Blizzards melt
beneath my stance
like dragons slain
by mighty lance.

Death, he flees
upon my sight,
he never knew
I hoard the light.

DRUNKEN

Now let's meet our drunken fucker
with a son and wife he loves to beat.
Which makes them so skittish and frightened,
though they used to be so gentle and so sweet.
I call him a drunken, sunken prick
because he truly isn't worth a lick.
But his family still prays with him,
stays with him...
...for flows the same blood in them within him.

His right hand he saves for his Tommy,
a kid he never wanted for one day.
His left is bruised and arthritic,
having done it's work on dear old wifey May.
His breath smells like rotten, spoiled gin,
he's cheated, and he's strayed, and loves to sin.
But his family still prays with him,
stays with him...
...for flows the same blood in them within him.

Now Tommy, he works like a service dog,
so loyal, and so faithful, and so steady.
With hopes his pops will soon return to work,
though he won't until he's damn well said he's ready.
And May, her job's a simple one:
keep her mouth shut and if need be, hide the gun.
But his family still prays with him,
stays with him...
...for flows the same blood in them within him.

This terror, it lasted forty years
until one day, the drunken fuck, he died.
It happened without a hint of ceremony,
Just one day, the drunken fuck, he died.
He left his son: debt, scars, disdain.
His wife: nightmares, scars, and pain, and pain.
But his family still prayed with him,
stayed with him...
...for flowed the same blood in them within him.

Under the ground, he sobered up,
then rose up from his grave in form of ghost.
He traveled long, and far and wide,
to see the ones he truly loved the most.
Now did he go back to visit wife and son?
Those that would have called him a loved one?
The family that prayed with him,
stayed with him...
...for flowed the same blood in them within him.

I'm afraid, dear friends, that's not what happened,
It's nowhere close to whom he went to see.
He went to see the bartender and concubine,
those who offered vice mixed with whiskey.
So who's the lesser in this tale?
The drunken fuck with life of lies and fail?
Or his family that prayed with him,
stayed with him...
...only 'cause their same blood was in him.

OUTRAGE

Outrage

is

an

unfair

default.

Out of rage

is

an

unfair

standard.

SOAKED

A walk on the beach
on a hot sunny day
the tide gently kissing
my toes.

Love is a wave
coming in hard and fast
taking my feet out.
My body left soaked.
And wet.
And cool.

Leaving me bewildered
and stunned
and joyful
and scared
and thrilled
and full
of fearful laughter.

NATURAL

The waves of sadness wash over me
rolling down my body with an icy wetness that numbs—
drenching me through.
I want to express my sadness,
but there is no space for that.
Not here,
in this city,
with these people.
They'll make you sad for feeling sad.
Like you've done something wrong.
Cheer up.

The clutch of grief strangles me,
hugging me with its unrelenting assertion—
an embrace that cannot be declined.
I want to express my grief,
but there is no space for that.
Not here,
in this city,
with these people.
They'll detach for fear of feeling grief.
Like you've done something wrong.
Move on.

The fires of anger sizzle my insides,
charring my heart and heating my skin—
an explosion locked in a box.
I want to express my anger,
but there is no space for that.
Not here,
in this city,
with these people.
They'll spit back anger from tasting your anger.
Like you've done something wrong.
Calm down.

So I go to the ocean to weep my sadness,
but the waves are no bigger than they were.

And I go to the mountains to let loose my grief,
but the snow does not melt into tears.

And I go to the desert to rage my anger,
but the earth is still, and does not quake.

Stalking the night for evidence of a world altered,
I find only

what's

natural.

DEATH

Death asked me, "Is it time to go?"
I thought that's something *he* should know,
for when he came the winds did blow,
and iced my trembling spine.

"You have a choice," he whispered shrill,
and pointed at my window sill,
his exit and my shattered will
were balanced on the line.

I said to him, "The offer's sound,
but I prefer feet on the ground,
now watch the door, it swings around,
don't let it hit your hind."

EDGE

Edge

is the ability

to withstand

every

single

skeptical

sideways

glance.

Life is a sucker-punch.

Our choices:

Crumble.

Acquiesce.

Fight back.

I'm on a bona fide path.
A path filled with virtuous things.
A path that is right,
a path pure and bright—
a path where I'll earn angel wings.

You're on a treacherous path.
A path that winds through the thorns.
A path that's a lark,
a path cold and dark—
a path where you'll grow devil horns.

We all think we're on the first path.
There's no way we're on number two.
We're too smart for that,
we're lions, not rats—
if you say otherwise, then screw you.

JOURNEY

If you tell me to enjoy the journey,

I'm going to make you carry my shit.

BE

In this moment

should I try

to be

a stronger person

or

a better student?

WAVE

A lake of glass
gentle
but unyielding
in its calm
runs
from my heart
to my back.

The water's calm
drapes over me
into me
through me
without permission
or consent.

Its navy surface
hints at
chilled depths
beyond light,
beyond night,
beyond sight.

Pull me out
of this stoic
venerable
intangible
hypothermic
peace.

Make a wave.
Will you?

A splash
a little splash
so I know
I'm still here
with you.

HERON

On a day so bright and vivid
I saw something bold and livid.
Something which I'll tell you evermore.
For this thing it was a blessing,
though it wrecked me, so distressing.
Something I still feel inside my core.

Though this day was bright and clear,
I took in something I still fear,
because of how it changed me through and through.
I witnessed life. I witnessed death.
I made a choice of who got breath.
And these actions birthed my soul anew.

Quietly I walked the shore.
I breathed the air it was so pure.
As my steps, they brought me straight ahead.
And on my path there were two things,
two creatures of which fate did bring,
two souls of which one would soon be dead.

This sight, it brought me none of joy:
a tall blue heron and a koi
were there amongst the surf and seaside spray.
The koi was dying, body flapping.
The heron perched, its wings were clapping,
proud and bold and boasting of its prey.

For the bird, it caught this meal.
It's feathers ruffled, shining teal,
while the orange koi was turning white.
And in that moment I grew cold,
yet simultaneously bold,
as two sides of me began to fight.

"Save the koi," my head did say.
"Frighten that huge bird away,
and place the fish right back into the lake.
For the koi, he cannot fight
and death will come with heron's bite.
To watch him die will make my heart so ache."

But then another side chimed in,
a thought with bitterness like gin,
a voice so gravely and full of spite:
"You'd deny this bird a feast?
Deny this victorious beast
the food that gives it energy for flight?"

And so I had to make a choice.
I had to listen to one voice.
I had to sentence one of them to death.
My heart it swelled and pulsed and pounded.
Wrenched and throbbed and ached and sounded
like a drum, while I grew short of breath.

I couldn't let a creature die.
I thought, "What kind of man am I?
To not fight for the lesser, helpless soul?"
I charged and swung my arms astray.
I scared the massive bird away!
As it hollered like some kind of troll.

But it was not so sure of flight.
It ebbed so harshly to the right.
Reluctant to put pressure on its wing.
An injured bird. It was not strong.
I thought it virile. I was wrong.
Imagine all that pain and suffering.

I approached my scaly friend,
its body shook, its back did bend.
"Don't worry, you'll go back into the sea."
I scooped him up into my palm,
and walked him to the water's calm.
I watched him swim, restored, alive and free.

"I saved a life," I reassured
the part of me who's mind was blurred
with images of the blue heron starved.

But then...
I saw it.

I stabbed myself with words of hate!
I had failed this test of fate!
My righteousness would damn my soul to hell.
For in the distance, with the bird,
some tiny, tiny creatures stirred.
The heron paced amongst a nest that fell.

Five starving chicks squeaked for the food
they hoped their mother had accrued.
But she had nothing but a broken limb.
The heron gazed a stare so solemn.
It froze my neck and spinal column.
For I knew the birds, their light would dim.

And on this day I felt the pangs
of lessons entering like fangs
that would leave no room for recompense.
For in choosing death or life
I felt the plunge just like a knife
into the everlasting void of consequence.

Still to this day, my sunken back
weighs heavy of this choice so black.
Oh how I wish this wound would someday heal.
But it shall not, instead he'll say
each and every single day:
"Sometimes, let the monster have his meal."

ACKNOWLEDGMENTS

Writing poetry is like bleeding out onto a page. These are the people who were kind enough to help me sharpen the knife.

Keegan Allen, Perri Cohn, Phoenix Conrad, Phil Gevaux, Rosa Nadine Xochimilco Gevaux, Camille Grenier, Gary Howard, Jeremy Howard, Lorin Howard, Meagan Lopez, Deborah Lurie, Willis Lurie, Lavena Mathrani, Jack Nolan, William Rowel, Michi Sellars, Satsuki Takahashi, Kaitlin Weichsel, Julisa Wilson, Karen Yee.

And so many, many more.

A novel by the author

Mortal Enemy - Legends of the Grim Reaper #1 is thrilling, chilling, and epic in scale. It is a relentless whirlwind of action and adventure. A saga of conflicted heroes and devious villains. A journey rife with darkness and struggle, yet also wicked humor.

Now available in print and ebook editions, and as an immersive audio experience that streams for free on many major platforms. Features an extraordinary cast of performers, multidimensional sound, cinematic-quality effects, and a spectacular orchestral score.

Narrated by Reid Scott (*Venom*) and Devin Kelley (*Frequency*). Performed by Eric Christian Olsen (*NCIS: Los Angeles*), Troian Bellisario (*Pretty Little Liars*), Chris Pine (*Wonder Woman*), Keegan Allen (*Pretty Little Liars*), Patrick J. Adams (*Suits*), Sarah Wright Olsen (*American Made*), Brett Dier (*Jane the Virgin*), Christa B. Allen (*Revenge*), Brendan Hines (*The Tick*), Adetokumboh M'Cormack (*Castlevania*), Jamie Harris (*The Prestige*), Robert Pine (*Frozen*), Neal Bledsoe (*The Man in the High Castle*), Robert Baker (*Supergirl*), and many more.

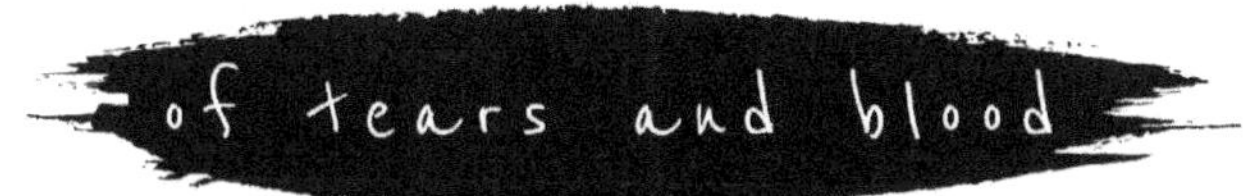

A podcast by the author

A journey into the creative consciousness of those who have spilled blood, sweat and tears relentlessly pursuing their craft.

Nicholas Ryan Howard unapologetically takes the most honest, direct, and unfiltered approach possible to the topic discovering alongside his guests the challenges—but also the joys—of creating.

Features interviews with some of the most prolific actors, comedians, musicians, chefs, directors, and artists on the planet, stretching from the United States to Europe and beyond.

Welcome to *Of Tears and Blood*, where we explore the raw truths of the creative process.

ABOUT THE AUTHOR

www.NicholasRyanH.com
@NicholasRyanH

Nicholas Ryan Howard is an author, philosopher, and expert in the field of Creativity. He was educated at The University of Southern California in Communications and trained as a Master Facilitator in Spiritual Psychology at the University of Santa Monica, where he later served as a Director. As a media producer and content creator he has worked on such properties as *The Bourne Identity*, *Harry Potter*, and *Star Wars*, and he is the visionary behind the epic *Legends of the Grim Reaper* saga as well as the podcast *Of Tears and Blood*. Currently he spends his time dreaming up new worlds, counseling individuals on their expansion of consciousness, consulting with organizations, and speaking around the globe.

www.ingramcontent.com/pod-product-compliance
Lightning Source LLC
Chambersburg PA
CBHW070809050426
42452CB00011B/1958

* 9 7 8 1 7 3 2 8 8 7 8 4 8 *